Haunted Dolls

Susan B. Katz

Lerner Publications • Minneapolis

T0015916

For Ginger, who was a comfort when things were scary

Lerner Publications Company
An imprint of Lerner Publishing Group, Inc.
241 First Avenue North
Minneapolis, MN 55401 USA

For reading levels and more information, look up this title at www.lernerbooks.com.

Main body text set in Billy Infant Regular. Typeface provided by SparkType.

Photo Editor: Annie Zheng

Library of Congress Cataloging-in-Publication Data

Names: Katz, Susan B., 1971- author.
Title: Haunted dolls / Susan B. Katz.
Description: Minneapolis, MN : Lerner Publications , [2023] | Series: Lightning bolt books
— That's scary! | Includes bibliographical references and index. | Audience: Ages 6-9 |
Audience: Grades 2-3 | Summary: "Kids around the world play with dolls—but what if a doll
was haunted? Some think dolls can have powers or even cause bad things to happen. This
scary-yet-fun book takes a look at spooky dolls!"— Provided by publisher.
Identifiers: LCCN 2022035733 (print) | LCCN 2022035734 (ebook) | ISBN 9781728491165
(library binding) | ISBN 9781728498621 (ebook)
Subjects: LCSH: Haunted dolls—Juvenile literature.
Classification: LCC BF1474.35 K38 2023 (print) | LCC BF1474.35 (ebook) | DDC 133.1—dc23/
eng/20220914

LC record available at https://lccn.loc.gov/2022035733
LC ebook record available at https://lccn.loc.gov/2022035734

Manufactured in the United States of America
1-53047-51065-11/28/2022

Table of Contents

Spooky Dolls

All around the world, children play with dolls. Most are sweet and fun to play with. But some can seem spooky!

Some people think dolls can have powers, make curses, or cause bad things to happen. Others think haunted dolls are watching them!

Some people blame haunted dolls for bad luck.

Haunted Dolls in Folklore

Stories passed from person to person are folklore. Stories about a doll named Annabelle started in the 1970s. Donna, a nursing student, got Annabelle from her mother.

Could Annabelle have written notes?

Donna and her roommate noticed that the doll didn't stay where Donna put it. It seemed to move by itself. They also found notes asking for help.

Another story is about a doll named Mandy. Mandy's owner said she heard the doll crying. She gave the doll to a museum. Workers there soon noticed their lunches disappearing!

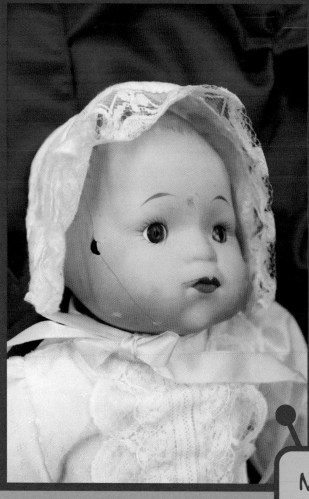

Mandy is a porcelain doll like this one.

Robert is a famous doll in a Florida museum. Stories say if visitors want to take his photo, they must ask Robert nicely or they will be cursed.

People visit Robert in Key West, Florida, at the Fort East Martello Museum.

EAST MARTELLO MUSEUM
Circa 1862
NATIONAL REGISTER·HISTORIC SITE
OPEN DAILY

Haunted Dolls around the World

Have you ever told a scary story by a campfire? Kids around the world like to tell scary stories. Some of them are about dolls.

One scary doll story comes from Japan. It started around 1918, when a young man bought a doll named Okiku for his little sister. A year later, she got ill and died.

A porcelain doll from Japan

Okiku is in a temple in Hokkaido, Japan.

The family built a shrine, or a place to remember their daughter. They placed the doll there. Then they saw that the doll's short hair grew past its shoulders!

Another story comes from Mexico. It's about a place called the Island of the Dolls. Long ago, people used to hide there from Spanish invaders.

The Island of the Dolls is south of Mexico City.

In the 1950s, a man living there started seeing ghosts. He collected over one thousand dolls to scare the ghosts away. The dolls are still there, and some say they are haunted!

Would you visit the Island of the Dolls?

Letta was found under the floorboards of an old house.

A man in Australia found a haunted doll in 1972. He discovered it under some floorboards. The doll scared dogs, and sometimes the man heard it screaming, "Letta me out!" He began calling it Letta.

Haunted Dolls in Books and On-Screen

Haunted dolls often appear in books, movies, and TV shows. Talky Tina was in the TV show *The Twilight Zone*. The doll is a gift to a young girl, but Talky Tina says spooky things to the girl's stepdad when the girl isn't around.

Goosebumps was a popular book series and TV show in the 1990s. The *Goosebumps* character Slappy is a ventriloquist's dummy. Slappy can turn humans into dummies.

Ventriloquists use their voices to make it seem as if dummies can talk.

Coraline is a story by Neil Gaiman. In the story, a girl meets a mother much like her own behind a secret door. But the mom has button eyes. She wants to sew buttons over the girl's eyes too.

Some people find button eyes creepy!

Many stories talk about haunted dolls. The stories can be fun to hear and share. Do you have a favorite tale about a haunted doll?

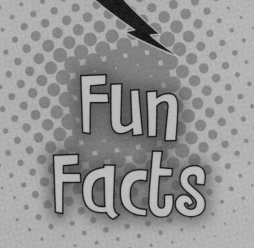

Fun Facts

- Some of the first dolls were made in Egypt around 2000 BCE.

- Baby dolls are popular now, but most antique dolls were made to look like adults.

- Doll hospitals fix broken dolls.

Dealing with Haunted Dolls

How do you get rid of a haunted doll? Some say the only way is to take it to an ocean and toss it into deep water. The power of the water will drown the doll and take away its evil curses.

Glossary

curse: bad luck or evil said to be caused by someone or something

dummy: a large puppet used in stage performances

folklore: stories passed from person to person

museum: a building that holds collections of objects

shrine: a place to pay your respects to someone or something

ventriloquist: a performer who uses their voice to make it seem as if dummies can talk

Learn More

Abdo, Kenny. *Ghosts.* Minneapolis: Fly!, 2020.

Britannica Kids: Ghost
https://kids.britannica.com/kids/article/ghost/574605

Britannica Kids: Toy
https://kids.britannica.com/kids/article/toy/399627

Carlson-Berne, Emma. *Mummies Around the World.* Minneapolis: Lerner Publications, 2024.

CBC Kids: "6 Spooky Things You Didn't Know about Ghosts"
https://www.cbc.ca/kids/articles/monsters-101-all-about-ghosts

Lassieur, Allison. *Scary Stuff.* Mankato, MN: Child's World, 2020.

Index

Photo Acknowledgments

Image credits: pixalot/iStock/Getty Images, p. 4; Sayan_Moongklang/iStock/Getty Images, p. 5; AmityPhotos/Alamy Stock Photo, p. 6; ibnu alias/Shutterstock, p. 7; val lawless/Shutterstock, p. 8; Derekeckley/Wikimedia Commons (CC BY-SA 4.0), p. 9; omgimages/iStock/Getty Images, p. 10; Ethan Jorge Fazon/EyeEm/Getty Images, p. 11; SeanPavonePhoto/iStock/Getty Images, p. 12; Walter Bibikow/Digital Vision/Getty Images, p. 13; David Espejo/Moment/Getty Images, p. 14; duncan1890/E+/Getty Images, p. 15; CBS Photo Archive/CBS/Getty Images, p. 16; Design Pics/Getty Images, p. 17; chromoff/Shutterstock, p. 18; Pixel-Shot/Shutterstock, p. 19.

Cover: Aubrey Hollopeter/Shutterstock.